Lovin My Daughter-In-Law

Create More Connection and Fun in Your Relationship with Others, Especially Your Daughter-In-Law

LeAnn Austin
Master Certified Life Coach & Teacher

© Copyright 2023 - All rights reserved.

The content contained within this book may not be reproduced, duplicated or transmitted without direct written permission from the author or the publisher.

Under no circumstances will any blame or legal responsibility be held against the publisher, or author, for any damages, reparation, or monetary loss due to the information contained within this book, either directly or indirectly.

Legal Notice:

This book is copyright protected. It is only for personal use. You cannot amend, distribute, sell, use, quote or paraphrase any part, or the content within this book, without the consent of the author or publisher.

Disclaimer Notice:

Please note the information contained within this document is for educational and entertainment purposes only. All effort has been executed to present accurate, up to date, reliable, complete information. No warranties of any kind are declared or implied. Readers acknowledge that the author is not engaged in the rendering of legal, financial, medical or professional advice. The content within this book has been derived from various sources. Please consult a licensed professional before attempting any techniques outlined in this book.

By reading this document, the reader agrees that under no circumstances is the author responsible for any losses, direct or indirect, that are incurred as a result of the use of the information contained within this document, including, but not limited to, errors, omissions, or inaccuracies.

PRAISE FOR
Lovin My Daughter-In-Law

Alyson Bray:
"Everything LeAnn does she puts her whole heart and soul into, and this book is no exception. LeAnn's personal stories are relatable, her illustrations are easy to understand, and her exercises are easy to follow. If you have a desire to improve your relationships with self or others, this book is an essential read. LeAnn's expertise, experience, and insight will guide readers to understand the importance of unconditional love more fully."

Candice Toone:
"LeAnn is THE definitive example of how to turn a painful daughter-in-law relationship into a loving one. She's THE go to guide to make that happen for you too."

Jenni Whiteley:
"After reading LeAnn's book, I am extremely motivated to use her DIL triangle--not just for creating better relationships with my own daughters-in-law, but with myself."

Lisa Van Otten:

"Written in an easy to understand, conversational manner, this book is filled with valuable bite-sized bits of information and actionable steps that will change the way you think about your relationships. Improving relationships is hard work. It is helpful to have a guide into changing your thoughts resulting in changing your relationship. Worth the read!"

Liz Bunker:

"*Lovin My Daughter-in-law* is not just for loving daughters-in-law, but any relationship you want to improve. Loaded with pearls of wisdom, LeAnn gently helps us grow, increasing our capacity for loving others as well as ourselves. A must read for anyone interested in finding more joy in life."

Shaina DeFichy:

"If you are a mother-in-law who wants to have a better relationship with their daughter-in-law this is THE book for you.

Loving my DIL is a fantastic book that is to the point and has the power to transform strained relationships into loving, supportive connections.

The advice, exercises and insights provided in this book are practical, compassionate, and incredibly effective.

The real-life stories and examples make it easy to relate and apply the advice to your own situation.

Throughout this book you will learn how to communicate better, understand your DIL's perspective, and even possibly build a bond that you never thought possible.

I highly recommend it to any mother-in-law looking to bridge the gap and create a more harmonious connection with their daughter-in-law."

For the mother-in-law who knows the relationship with her daughter-in-law can be even better

Hey Beautiful Reader~

Thank you for purchasing my book. I love a good read that opens up my mind to new ideas and experiences.

If you're looking for an inspiring read, and ways to create more fun and connection in your relationship with others, especially you're daughter-in-law, then you're in the right place.

If you'd like this book to be a life-changing experience, I invite you to download the free book resource that goes with it.

I love to take notes when I'm learning new information, and this worksheet may be used side by side with the book to practice and reinforce some of the skills I teach.

Scan the QR code and enter your email for a Free Book Resource Download:

Reading Companion or go to
https://leannaustin.com/book-resource/

Here's to connection, fun, and love~

CONTENTS

INTRODUCTION	1
TRIANGLE SIDE 1: Discover	5
TRIANGLE INSIDE 1: Circumstance & Thought	11
TRIANGLE SIDE 2: Intuition	17
TRIANGLE INSIDE 2: Feeling	21
TRIANGLE SIDE 3: Love	27
TRIANGLE INSIDE 3: Action & Result	33
CONCLUSION	37
ACKNOWLEDGEMENTS	39
ABOUT THE AUTHOR	41
RESOURCES	42

INTRODUCTION

I have two daughters-in-law, and they are amazing, but I haven't always thought that.

I met one of my daughters-in-law over 8 years ago, and I was not very kind to her. I was resistant to getting to know her. I thought the relationship between her and my son was too serious. I was even judgmental about what clothes she wore.

With my other daughter-in-law, whom I've known for over 6 years now, I was concerned that she hadn't had a job in high school or college. I questioned if she knew the value of work and whether she would be able to secure a job. I had so many judgments about her, and I really didn't know her at all.

Then there was me as a daughter-in-law. I experienced a difficult relationship with my mother-in-law for over 20 years. I felt that she was critical of everything I did or didn't do, and that she made no effort to get to know me. It was interesting to realize that I was doing the same thing when I first met my daughters-in-law.

Thankfully, I discovered life coaching. I will be forever grateful that someone recommended Jody Moore's podcast to me. I wasn't even familiar with podcasts at the time but figured out how to listen and was immediately hooked. Soon after, I

INTRODUCTION

attended Jody's weeklong Be Bold Masters event. During the week, I excitedly called my husband and told him I wanted to attend Brooke Castillo's The Life Coach School and get certified to become a life coach.

Learning the Brooke Castillo Model, which I'll explain in this book, opened a whole new world for me. I figured out that I can put any situation into the Model and gain so much awareness and understanding of what is happening in my mind.

As I strengthened my mental and emotional muscles, I learned how to navigate the relationships I had with myself and with others much better.

My relationships with my daughters-in-law and my mother-in-law greatly improved as I practiced all the new knowledge I had acquired. These amazing women hadn't changed during the process, but the way I saw them did. I came to truly appreciate, adore, and admire each one of them.

Because of my experiences, I am passionate about the mother-in-law and daughter-in-law relationship. I also love acronyms. I created an acronym to increase the love you feel for your daughter-in-law, mother-in-law, or really anybody. I will use daughter-in-law examples in this book, but you can apply this to any relationship you'd like.

What is a relationship anyway?

Relationships are simply our thoughts about another person. You might have a daughter-in-law that drives you nuts, but someone else might think she is the best person ever. How can two people experience the same person so differently? Your daughter-in-law didn't change. The other person has a different perception of your daughter-in-law because the other person has different thoughts. That person's relationship with your daughter-in-law depends on the person's thoughts about her.

Remember, your relationship with anyone is determined by your thoughts about them.

Why is this so crucial for you to understand? Because if our relationships are our thoughts about someone else, that is great news, we are in control of how we think. We can tweak our thoughts, no one else determines what we choose to believe.

Combining my Daughter-in-law Acronym with the Model, that I'll teach you in this book, has helped me and hundreds of my clients to create more fun and genuine connections with their daughter-in-law and others they care about.

Get ready to improve your relationship with your daughter-in-law or anyone – let's begin by thinking D-I-L.

Lovin My Daughter-In-Law
DIL Acronym

Discover

TRIANGLE SIDE 1
Discover

D is for Discover

Our family saved extra money for two years to buy dirt for a garden we wanted to plant. A big pile of soil was finally dumped in our driveway. My husband, myself, and our four young boys went to work. With wheelbarrows and shovels, we magically transformed the dirt into a garden.

The boys each picked something they would plant, and I tried a few veggies and fruits I'd been thinking about. We sowed tomatoes, squash, peas, sweet potatoes, and peppers. We watered and weeded, and soon little sprouts began to pop out of the ground. It was so fun to watch. Soon we were eating the fruits and vegetables that had only been seeds a few months earlier.

Everything seemed to be growing well except for the sweet potatoes. Little green shoots were popping out from the soil everywhere else, except for the mounds of dirt where we planted the sweet potatoes.

I discussed my concern with a friend and explained that I couldn't figure out why my sweet potatoes wouldn't grow. She

TRIANGLE SIDE 1: DISCOVER

smiled at me and said, "sweet potatoes grow under the ground, not above the ground." What? My mind was blown. I quickly ran out to the garden and started digging. I *discovered* the most beautiful, orange sweet potatoes under all that dirt. There were a bunch of them, and I was beyond excited!

Isn't it interesting when I knew nothing about sweet potatoes growing under the ground and then *discovered* that they did, how exciting and fun that was?

Discover means to: find out, learn, get curious

Ask yourself:

What can you *discover* about your daughter-in-law?

What about her may surprise you?

For example, one of my daughters-in-law likes Reese's Peanut Butter Cups and fishing. She doesn't like cold weather or doing laundry. My other daughter-in-law likes soda runs and speaking Portuguese. She doesn't like trying new foods or dark winters. They both have an eye for beautiful things and enjoy shopping. They love their dogs, and they each love their husbands, my sons.

Think about ways you could *discover* more about your daughter-in-law.

What does your son see in her?

Check to see that you're coming from curiosity - that there IS something worth seeing in your daughter-in-law that your son already sees, rather than sarcasm - that son is an idiot for loving her.

When we're curious, it opens our minds to so much more understanding and increases the love we feel for our daughter-in-law.

"So, LeAnn, how do I *discover* more about my daughter-in-law?" you might ask.

Maybe it's simply asking her questions.

Maybe it's talking to your son or grandkids about things she likes.

Once in a while, I'll ask my kids (which includes my daughters-in-law) what their favorite kind of veggie, treat, music, etc. is?

If you want to make the relationship with your daughter-in-law even better than it is – *Discover* everything you can about her.

There's a quote that I heard years ago that I love: **"You either love someone or you don't understand them."** Now there may be a few people in your life that you don't want to understand or feel love for, and that's okay. This book is to help with all relationships that you do want to improve.

The best way to understand a daughter-in-law is to *discover* everything you can about her. When you understand someone, it's so much easier to love them.

One more idea that may be helpful when *discovering* more about your daughter-in-law is a science experiment.

My daughter-in-law, Sarah is finishing up her master's degree, and she enjoys doing research. So, if I wanted to improve our relationship, and I was trying to *discover* more about her, then what...

TRIANGLE SIDE 1: DISCOVER

What if I thought about the endeavor as a research paper or a science experiment? My whole objective would be to *discover* everything I could about this amazing human.

Even if I didn't think that she's amazing all the time, I know that every person on the planet is 100% loveable and valuable all the time, no exceptions. I know that there is no hierarchy of humans, no one is "better" than another.

If I understand that and look at the person I'm trying to *discover* more about from that perspective, it's much easier to learn more about them.

Then, each time I'm with one of my daughters-in-law, or interacting with them via texts or calls or whatever, I'm *discovering* things about her – what she likes and doesn't like, what her hobbies are, what gets her excited or makes her sad.

Why is it helpful to be in a *discover* mode and how will this help your relationship?

You're going to feel so much better when you come from curiosity and *discovery*, rather than judgment and criticism.

What is it that you don't understand about your daughter-in-law? Let's *discover* more!

DIL Activity:

Discover 3 new things about your daughter-in-law.

Lovin My Daughter-In-Law
DIL Acronym

Discover
Circumstance
Thought

TRIANGLE INSIDE 1
Circumstance & Thought

A Circumstance is a fact. And a thought….maybe not?

Forty-plus years ago, I would drive with my grandpa up the mountain to the dump. Grandma would send us with yummy Hostess treats, and we'd travel up the windy road to the top in the truck filled with items that needed to be discarded.

My grandpa would back up to the end of the cliff. (Many times I was convinced we would fall off the edge because he'd get so close). Then he'd lift the bed of the truck and dump everything out. He'd pull forward a little bit, take his broom, and sweep out anything that was stuck in the corners.

This is what I love to do with my mind, "dump" everything out. So I can look at what's there, then decide which thoughts I want to keep and which ones I want to dump. I call this a thought dump.

TRIANGLE INSIDE 1: CIRCUMSTANCE & THOUGHTS

DIL Activity:

Step 1: Grab a piece of paper and pen. For the next 5 minutes, write down everything you think about your daughter-in-law. Everything. Get it all out. (You can throw it away after, so no worries about someone seeing it). This exercise is to simply dump everything out of your beautiful brain. Don't worry about grammar or spelling, just write.

Step 2: Now go back through the words that you dumped out and circle all the phrases that are actually true. What are the facts that everyone would agree with about your daughter-in-law? I'm talking very specific and factual here. Truths you could go into a courtroom with, and everyone would agree with them. Facts or circumstances are things we can't change. For example, we can't change where daughter-in-law was born or how old she is in this exact moment. We can't change the date of their anniversary or where they first met.

Notice that your thought dump consisted mainly of things that are not completely factual, they are simply thoughts. Some people may agree with them, but some may not.

The fascinating thing about distinguishing between thoughts and circumstances is, we can't change the circumstances (the facts), but we can absolutely tweak what we're thinking.

Step 3: All right, you've dumped out all of your thoughts about your daughter-in-law. You've gone back through your list and circled the phrases that are actually true. Now, from the words not circled, pick out one of the thoughts that seems to be problematic, and let's take a closer look at that thought.

LOVIN MY DAUGHTER-IN-LAW

We're going to start wiggling it. I love to think of this as like wiggling a tooth. We're simply loosening it. We're realizing that maybe it's not as factual as we think. To do this, ask yourself the following questions as you *discover*...

What about this thought isn't true?

What am I making this thought mean?

What is the opposite of this thought?

For example:

Here's a portion of a daughter-in-law thought dump from one of my clients:

Daughter-in-law didn't come to our family event,
I don't understand why she doesn't spend time with us,
what have I done that makes her not want to come,
she is so selfish and never thinks about my feelings,
we have a dinner scheduled for next week and I don't know if she'll come,
I don't know if I even want her to come,

If we reread back through this, what is actually true that everyone would agree with?

"Didn't come to our family event" and "dinner scheduled for next week". Everything else is simply thoughts.

Now we can't change the facts, but we can tweak what we're thinking. Let's pick out one of the many thoughts to wiggle, such as...

"She is so selfish."

TRIANGLE INSIDE 1: CIRCUMSTANCE & THOUGHTS

Let's *discover* more about that thought.

What about this thought isn't true...well, daughter-in-law isn't selfish ALL the time, there are sometimes when she's not selfish. Selfish means lacking consideration for others. Are there times when daughter-in-law has been concerned about someone else?

What am I making this thought mean...that she doesn't care about me and only thinks about herself. Maybe there are times that she thinks about me.

What is the opposite of this thought...She is selfless. She thinks about others. She loves my son and grandkids. *Discover* all the ways daughter-in-law is selfless rather than selfish.

You may be saying, wait LeAnn, I don't want to change what I'm thinking about my daughter-in-law. You don't have to. I simply want to show you that what you're thinking about is going to reflect in your relationship with your daughter-in-law. So, *discovering* and bringing awareness to your thoughts is key to getting the results that you truly desire.

You may be thinking that daughter-in-law is getting off scot-free while I'm changing who I am. This could be true, and maybe not. When you start to tweak your thoughts that aren't serving you, it is so helpful to YOU, not just your daughter-in-law.

Now we've got one side of the triangle, both inside and out.

Quick Recap:

Discover everything possible about your daughter-in-law – find out, learn more, and get curious.

Discover what is happening inside YOUR brain.

Dump everything out onto paper, go back through and *discover* what is a thought and what is a circumstance.

Pick one of the thoughts that is not serving you and start wiggling it (what is not true about that thought?).

DIL Activity:

Write down everything you think about your daughter-in-law, and then wiggle/explore one of those thoughts.

Just like you discovered 3 new things about your daughter-in-law, now you're discovering what you're thinking about her.

Lovin My Daughter-In-Law
DIL Acronym

Discover

Circumstance

Thought

Intuition

TRIANGLE SIDE 2
Intuition

I is for Intuition

*I*ntuition *is defined as: the ability to understand something immediately, without the need for conscious reasoning. It's instinctive, it's that feeling in your gut.*

Think about times in your life when you've felt that *intuition* to say or do something. This happens to me often. A thought, a prompt, *intuition*, or whatever you want to call it will pop into my mind. It may be to send a text or call someone. It may be to say something in a conversation or to not say something. It may be to do or not do a specific thing. Whatever it is, I'm always glad when I listen to my *intuition*. Sometimes my *intuition* is totally random, but if it's coming from compassion and love, I try to listen and do it.

What's your *intuition* telling you about your daughter-in-law? Listen to it.

This happened to me a couple of years ago. I decided I was going to attend a faith-based sex retreat, and I kept feeling like I should invite my daughters-in-law. But then I'd second guess

TRIANGLE SIDE 2: INTUITION

myself and think, "they are not going to want to go to a sex retreat with their mother-in-law". However, I kept thinking about it and my *intuition* kept telling me to ask them. I felt it would be beneficial to everyone. I figured the worst that could happen was they'd tell me no, and it would not be a big deal if they did. We could then find something else to do together.

I finally asked both of my daughters-in-law, and they both wanted to go. We went and had an amazing time together. I'm so glad I listened to my *intuition* and invited them to attend with me, even though I felt uncomfortable in the asking. Doing things that don't feel great in the moment, but that we know deep down we want intuitively, strengthens our ability to listen to our *intuition* and act accordingly.

That experience with my daughters-in-law strengthened our relationship in countless ways. We talked, laughed, cried and danced. We learned a lot, and they taught me things that I wish I had known 30 years ago. We had our make-up and hair done, we took pictures, and we spent time outdoors walking and running together. I'll forever be thankful that I followed my *intuition* and invited them to that faith-based sex retreat with me.

There have been other times when I didn't listen to my *intuition* and that's okay too. It's a skill I'm practicing. The more I try it out, and sometimes feel uncomfortable doing it, the better I get at figuring it out and showing up as the mother-in-law I want to be.

Sometimes listening to my *intuition* is saying no. Maybe your daughter-in-law wants you to pick up one of the grandkids, but you already have things going on at that time. If you don't want to do it or it doesn't work with your schedule, it's okay to say no.

Do what you feel good about, whatever is intuitive to you. We don't have to do everything our daughter-in-law wants us to do. Sometimes that means setting some boundaries about what you're willing and not willing to do. Setting boundaries is listening to your *intuition*.

Just like the good old oxygen mask on yourself first analogy that we hear on the airplane, when we take care of ourselves first and listen to our *intuition*, it is so much easier to show up and care for those around us.

Why is listening to your *intuition* going to help the relationship?

Because you'll know you are coming from love and compassion no matter what your daughter-in-law says or does. Learn to trust your *intuition*, even though it may be uncomfortable.

I never regret listening to and acting upon my *intuition*.

DIL Activity:

What is your *intuition* telling you about your daughter-in-law, and how are you listening?

Lovin My Daughter-In-Law
DIL Acronym

Discover
Circumstance
Thought
Feeling
Intuition

TRIANGLE INSIDE 2
Feeling

What do you feel when you think about your daughter-in-law?

Some of you may be very in tune with what you're feeling, and others not so much. In 2018, when I started listening to Jody Moore's podcast and was just learning what a life coach was, I was introduced to the importance of feelings.

I grew up with three brothers (no sisters) and I had four boys (no girls), so I was not familiar with family environments where there was lots of girl talk or expression of feelings. This was a whole new concept for me. It's been very beneficial for me to first understand that feelings are simply vibrations in our body caused by what we're thinking.

When I first met one of my daughters-in-law, I noticed a feeling of irritation arise. It was very uncomfortable, and I didn't really understand feelings or know what to do with them. Life coaching taught me the skill of feeling that has helped me in all my relationships. I know that becoming more aware of your

TRIANGLE INSIDE 2: FEELING

feelings can help in your relationships as well, give it a try and let me know what you think.

This awareness and breathing into a feeling are how we allow feelings. And when we allow our emotions/feelings and understand that they are coming from what we're thinking, then we can start moving in the direction we want to go.

When we resist or react to our emotions, they keep coming back. Feelings want to be seen, and when we push something away, it returns and is often stronger. "What we resist persists."

Take a few minutes and notice what you're feeling right now.

I like to put my hand on my heart and simply breathe into it. Then I describe my feeling by asking myself these questions:

Where is the feeling in my body?
What is its shape, texture, temperature?
Is it solid, transparent, or something else?
Does it move, vibrate, or sit still?
What else do you notice about the feeling?

Pretend like you are the examiner telling someone everything you possibly can about what this feels like in your body as if they've never felt this before.

My coach Brooke Castillo taught me the visual of a beach ball. Imagine a feeling as a beach ball that you are holding or that is sitting by you in the water. Notice when you try to push the beach ball down, avoid it, or hide it, it takes a lot of effort and eventually something is going to slip. When it does, that beach ball pops up out of the water with a lot of force.

The same is true with our feelings. Did you know that the worst thing that can happen to us is a negative emotion? We do or don't do things to feel better. Everything we do is because of how we think it will make us feel.

What we think about our daughter-in-law brings up lots of feelings for us. Sometimes we think.... she's taken away my son, she doesn't know how to raise my grandkids, she isn't trying to be a part of our family, and on and on.

Notice how it feels when you're thinking about one of these things. You may be like, well LeAnn, it's true. But take a step back and think about this. When I'm thinking this thought, is it helping me create more fun and connection with my daughter-in-law?

You may feel frustrated, irritated, or even devastated when thinking about your daughter-in-law. Take some time to really feel that in your body, and then notice what you're thinking that is creating that feeling of devastation or whatever the feeling is for you.

As you're becoming more aware of what is happening in your beautiful mind, and accepting where you're at, the judgment starts to lessen for both her and you. You want to get really good at allowing your feelings and letting them be there, rather than pushing them away or reacting to them.

When we truly feel and process our emotions, tweaking our thinking becomes so much easier. You can start to wiggle your thoughts and realize that maybe they're not quite as true as you originally thought, as your feeling is shifting to another vibration in your body.

TRIANGLE INSIDE 2: FEELING

DIL Activity:

Pause and discover what you're feeling when you're thinking about your daughter-in-law.

Take 3-5 minutes to really feel the emotion you are noticing and describe it.

This practice of feeling rather than resisting your emotions will create more connection with yourself and your daughter-in-law.

Lovin My Daughter-In-Law
DIL Acronym

Discover — Circumstance, Thought
Intuition — Feeling
Love

TRIANGLE SIDE 3

Love

L is for Love

I love to ask myself the question, what would *love* do? If you were feeling *love*, what would you do? Sometimes *love* is saying no, sometimes *love* is setting boundaries, but *love* is always telling the truth.

Love is a big part of relationships. But remember, *love* is a feeling that comes from our thoughts about another person. If we have loving thoughts about our daughter-in-law, then we'll feel *love* for her. This goes for the daughter-in-law's feelings too. She doesn't love us because of what we do or don't do. She feels *love* for us because of what she thinks about us.

This is something we have no control over. We can't change the way another human thinks or feels, but we can choose what we think or feel, simply by gaining more awareness around what we're thinking about our daughter-in-law that's keeping us from feeling *love* for her.

This goes right back to Discover & Intuition: Once we become aware of the thoughts that are blocking us from feeling *love* for our

TRIANGLE SIDE 3: LOVE

daughter-in-law, then we get to decide whether we want to keep them or tweak them.

Try this again...

Dump out of your mind all the thoughts you have about your daughter-in-law.

Write down everything that comes to mind – don't filter it, just write (no one else needs to see this and you can throw it away when you're done).

Once you've written everything you can think of, start with the thought that's bothering you most.

For example....

When thinking about your daughter-in-law, you may have written that "she's taking away my son."

You may be like, hey LeAnn it's true. It is a circumstance and not a thought. We don't get to see our son very often. We don't have a relationship like we used to, we don't get to see our grandkids as much as we'd like, and so many other things.

Many people may agree with you too, but not everyone. "She's taking away my son" is a thought that with practice and *love* can be tweaked into something that may be more useful to think. Your daughter-in-law might be taking him away – maybe they moved because of her, but does thinking that thought get you the relationship you want with your daughter-in-law?

Let's wiggle this a little more...simply look at that thought "she's taking away my son." Does that help you feel more love for your daughter-in-law? Probably not. It may feel terrible and frustrating and create anger for you.

And sometimes we do want to feel all those things about other people. That's completely normal and part of being human. Life is about feeling all the things. Whatever feeling you're experiencing when you think that thought, pause for a few minutes, and really feel it in your body.

Ask yourself the feeling questions that I mentioned before. Truly allow the frustration or anger to be there.

Where is it in my body?
What is its shape, texture, temperature?
Is it solid, transparent, or something else?
Does it move, vibrate, or sit still?
What else do you notice about the feeling?

Pretend like you are the examiner telling someone everything you possibly can about what this feels like in your body as if they've never felt this before.

(I like to put my hand on my heart and simply breathe into it. Then I describe my feeling to myself, noting all the things I'm feeling in my body.)

After experiencing whatever vibration you notice in your body, as well as a feeling of release or readiness, then let's go into discovery mode and ask yourself…

Is there any way you could be wrong about the thought "she's taking away my son"?

TRIANGLE SIDE 3: LOVE

I'm guessing there's a reason your son is with this girl. And sometimes the mere fact that your son loves her is reason enough for us to *discover* things to *love* about her too.

When you believe that your daughter-in-law is "taking away my son", you find all the evidence to support that – you're judgmental of her and yourself, you may withdraw from the situation, or tiptoe around trying to please her, and you're waiting for the next thing to go wrong.

When you think "she's taking away my son", then what ends up happening is you're "taking away yourself" in how you show up. Sometimes you hide or play small. Often you don't listen to your *intuition*. Ask yourself if you're *loving* and taking care of yourself, and giving your daughter-in-law a chance to see you for who you really are?

This came up for me a few years ago. Some of my boys and a daughter-in-law were home and we were all having dinner. They got up as soon as their food was gone and left the table, going to do something else. I was frustrated and a little mad. I noticed myself not wanting to say anything because my daughter-in-law was there, but then I thought wait, she's part of our family and I'm going to treat her like that. She may not like me sometimes and that's okay. I know my boys don't like me sometimes either, and there are times that I don't like them. That's part of being a human. Thankfully in that moment, I asked myself the question: What would love do?

I hollered at all the kids to come and help me clean up. And then the next time we were all together, I gave each of them a night to oversee dinner.

LOVIN MY DAUGHTER-IN-LAW

I don't want to go on vacation or have my family come over and think that I take care of all the meals. I want us all to share that experience together. The *loving* thing for me is everyone takes turns cooking and cleaning up when we're together.

P.S. I highly recommend taking turns cooking and cleaning up for so many reasons. Give your kids the opportunity to share foods they like, be responsible for making and cleaning up a family meal, and sharing the workload when everyone is together.

Whenever something comes up with your daughter-in-law, think about this question. What would *love* do?

DIL Activity:

Ask "What would *love* do?" each time you have an interaction with your daughter-in-law.

Lovin My Daughter-In-Law
DIL Acronym

- **Love**
  - Action
  - Result
- **Discover**
  - Circumstance
  - Thought
- **Intuition**
  - Feeling

TRIANGLE INSIDE 3
Action & Result

Are you walking on eggshells and not getting the results you want with your daughter-in-law?

What we are feeling fuels our **actions**. Notice that what you do and don't do depends on what you're feeling. This is why feelings really matter.

If you're feeling unsure around your daughter-in-law; maybe you withdraw, you hesitate to do things, you're more quiet than normal, or you have judgments for her and for yourself. All these actions come when you're feeling unsure thinking thoughts like: "My daughter-in-law is hard to please," or "She's doing it wrong."

What about feeling *love*? What do you do when you're feeling *love*? You listen, you're mindful, you're interested, you engage in conversation or an activity with your daughter-in-law.

This really goes back to our Thoughts and Feelings. Pay attention to what you're doing and observe what you're thinking and feeling that is fueling your actions.

TRIANGLE INSIDE 3: ACTION & RESULT

The last part of the Model is the **result**. What is happening right now, that is creating the disconnect with your daughter-in-law?

We often think the result is because of the circumstance (that we talked about on the Discover side of our triangle), but the result of what is happening in our lives is because of our thoughts about it.

For example...

We've talked about the 5 parts of the Model and the inside of our triangle. This is what it would look like if we took one of the thoughts we're thinking from our thought dump and put it into a model.

Circumstance: Grandson's Birthday Party, Daughter-in-law did not ask me to plan or help with the party

Thought: She is very rude.

Feeling: irritated

Actions: don't get excited about the party, very quiet and reserved, stay in the corner and don't participate in the games, think about all the things that daughter-in-law is doing wrong

Result: I am rude and not showing up as the mother-in-law I want to be.

Often, we think the problem is the **Circumstance**. But what is causing us to feel and do the things we're doing is our **Thought**.

In this example, we feel irritated and do all the actions mentioned, because we're thinking "Daughter-in-law is very rude." We think it's because daughter-in-law didn't ask us to plan and help with our grandson's party, but that's simply the facts of what happened. Another mother-in-law might be thrilled that they didn't have to plan or help with the party and could just show up. However, because we're thinking, "she is very rude," our result ends up with us being rude which we can see from our actions.

Whatever we're thinking shows up in our actions and will eventually end up as our result. That's why we want to pay attention to our thoughts because they create our results.

Let's stop giving the circumstance (the facts) so much power. We can't change the circumstances and when we're trying to, we're just fighting with reality. Byron Katie says, *"When you argue with reality, you lose, but only 100% of the time."*

DIL Activity:

Let's put this all together and you create your own Model about your daughter-in-law.

Circumstance: write down the facts of the situation

Thought: write down just one thought (short phrase) of what you're thinking about the circumstance

Feeling: What are you feeling when you're thinking that thought? Choose a one-word emotion that you're feeling in your body.

Actions: What are all the actions you are doing and not doing when you are feeling_____ and thinking_____?

TRIANGLE INSIDE 3: ACTION & RESULT

You can put as many actions and inactions as you'd like, as well as what you're thinking about and telling others.

<u>Result:</u> What is the result? Remember this supports the actions and relates to the thought you're thinking.

When you take your own unique situation and put it in this 5-part model (the inside of our triangle), you gain so much leverage over the situation. You're able to understand why you're feeling the way you are because of the thought you're thinking. There's nothing wrong with any thought we have. Using the model simply helps us to be aware that the thought creates our feeling, which fuels our actions and creates our results. If we want to change our actions and results, we need to tweak what we're thinking.

CONCLUSION

You now know the three action steps to my DIL acronym (Discover, Intuition, Love). Implementing even one of these actions will greatly improve your relationship with your daughter-in-law.

You can now take any situation and put it into the Model (the inside of our triangle – Circumstance, Thought, Feeling, Action, Result). Putting your unique situations into the model will bring awareness to your daughter-in-law's situations, thus giving you the power to change what is happening if you want to.

I encourage you to use these tools that you now have in your tool belt and practice them. However, like anything else, it doesn't do much good if the tools sit on the shelf and we don't use them. Pick one of them, try it, mess it up, and try it again.

If you want to improve your relationship with your daughter-in-law, there's not a perfect path where everyone gets along and is happy all the time. It's challenging and hard, we get frustrated and angry. Sometimes we feel that we must walk on eggshells and not be ourselves. That is not true. Your relationships can be different and even better than you imagine.

CONCLUSION

Envision the freedom and joy of skipping in and being yourself, rather than tiptoeing around your daughter-in-law (or anyone you care about).

Imagine spending time with your son and his family feeling love and joy, rather than frustration and judgment.

You can make that happen and now's the time. This book has given you my DIL acronym – 3 words that can change everything. You have an awareness tool (the Model) to use in any situation. You have real life examples and activities that matter. Use these tools to strengthen your mental and emotional muscles, and you will feel more love than ever before.

ACKNOWLEDGEMENTS

Jeff: for believing in me and cheering me on. Love the life we are creating together.

Ron & Helen: for being the best parents ever and supporting me in whatever I do.

Brandon, Kurtis, Nick, and Justin: for the incredible blessing each one of you is to me, and the gift of being your mom.

Sarah, Kristen, and my future daughters-in-law: for loving my boys, and giving me the opportunity to be a mother-in-law and have beautiful daughters in my life.

My Life Coaches: for coaching and teaching me countless treasures, and completely changing my life for the better.

All of My Clients past, present, and future: for sharing your heart and vulnerable stories with me. What an honor to strengthen the love you feel for yourself and others together.

Friends and Family: for your kindness, love, and connection. I'm so blessed.

ABOUT THE AUTHOR

LeAnn Austin is a Master Certified Life Coach and creator of Lovin My Daughter-in-law Podcast and Connection Crew Program. Her mission is to help people create more connection and fun in their relationships, especially with their daughter-in-law.

LeAnn is a certified trauma-informed, faith-based, and weightloss coach, and she coaches and instructs at The Life Coach School. LeAnn taught school for many years and facilitates classes to strengthen emotional resilience.

When LeAnn is not coaching, teaching, or podcasting, you can find her enjoying the outdoors, eating smoked meat, walking or running with her dog, getting strong enough to do a pull-up, and connecting with friends and family.

RESOURCES

Free Book Resource Download: Reading Companion
https://leannaustin.com/book-resource/

This worksheet may be used side by side with the book to practice and reinforce some of the skills I teach you.

LeAnn's Website
https://leannaustin.com/

The One Question
https://leannaustin.com/onequestion/

One Question that you can ask yourself anytime you're thinking about or struggling with your daughter-in-law. This One Question will greatly improve your relationship with your daughter-in-law RIGHT NOW – Instant download.

Lovin My Daughter-in-law Podcast
https://leannaustin.com/podcast/

Short and simple insights and ideas about love and strengthening relationships.

Weekly Wednesday Wins Email
https://leannaustin.com/wednesday-wins/

Wednesday email with short and impactful love and relationship information and questions to ponder.

LOVIN MY DAUGHTER-IN-LAW

Social Media – Instagram, Facebook, YouTube, TikTok
https://www.instagram.com/LeAnnAustinCoaching/
https://www.facebook.com/LeAnnAustinCoaching
https://www.tiktok.com/@leannaustincoaching
https://www.youtube.com/channel/UCQ9Lm7bLhbhQ5hIo2TCnJuw

Connection Crew Program
https://leannaustin.com/register/

If you're ready to create more connection and fun in your relationships, Connection Crew Program will show you how.

One to One Coaching
https://leannaustin.com/one-to-one-coaching/

Create results that you never thought possible through coaching/mentoring together one to one, working exclusively with a master certified, weightloss, and trauma informed coach.

Printed in Great Britain
by Amazon